PYTHON ASSOCIATES:

A TEENAGERS GUIDEBOOK FOR CODING

Contents

3

5

A Tomfoolery and Simple Presentation

Programming could appear to be an overwhelming undertaking, however with Python, a cordial and flexible programming language, getting everything rolling is a breeze, particularly for youngsters who are anxious to jump into the universe of coding. You'll learn how to set up your environment, write your first Python program, and get started on an exciting journey of discovery and creativity in this guide.

1st Chapter: Prologue to Python

Welcome to the universe of Python! The programming language Python is well-known for its readability and simplicity. It resembles learning another dialect, however rather than words and sentences, you'll be working with code to make astounding things on your PC. Things being what they are, the reason would it be a good idea for you to learn Python?

It's suitable for beginners: Python is planned in view of fledglings. Its linguistic structure is straightforward, pursuing it an ideal decision for youngsters who are simply beginning their coding experience.

Versatility: Python is utilized in a variety of fields, including data science, artificial intelligence, and web development. Learning Python opens up a plethora of career and project possibilities.

Local area and Assets: Python has an enormous and strong local area.

You can get assistance from a lot of resources, tutorials, and even other kids learning Python.

Section 2:

Setting Up Your Environment You must set up your coding environment before you can begin writing code. It resembles setting up your work area prior to beginning a craftsmanship project.

2.1 Installing Python Python can be installed on a computer with minimal effort. Visit the authority Python site (python.org) and explore to the "Downloads" segment. There are numerous editors to browse, and some are explicitly intended for youngsters. Two famous decisions are:

Thonny: Thonny is a fledgling accommodating Python IDE (Coordinated Improvement Climate). It is simple to use and has a straightforward interface for writing and running Python code.

Mu: Mu is another youngster accommodating code proofreader intended to make learning Python fun. It has features designed specifically for beginners and a straightforward interface.

Pick the one you see as generally agreeable, and we should continue on toward the thrilling part - composing your most memorable Python program!

Part 3: Greetings, World!

The custom in writing computer programs is to begin with a basic program that prints the expression "Hi, World!" to the screen. This assists you with guaranteeing that your current circumstance is set up accurately and that you're prepared to begin coding.

Type the following code into a new file using your preferred code editor:

python
Duplicate code
print("Hello, World!")
Presently, save your document with a ".py" expansion, for instance, "hello.py". Run your program, and presto! Your first Python program has just been written and run.

How to Crack the Code:

print(): In Python, there is a function called this that shows the contents of the parentheses on the screen.

"Hello, everyone!": This is a text string. You can change the text inside the statements to print anything you need.

Congratulations! You are currently formally a Python developer. In the following sections, we'll investigate factors, information types, and additional astonishing ideas that will engage you to make much cooler projects. The excursion has recently started, and the conceivable outcomes are inestimable. Blissful coding!

Prologue to Python

What is Python?

Python is a strong, undeniable level programming language known for its effortlessness and comprehensibility. It was made by Guido van Rossum and first delivered in 1991. Python's plan theory underscores code meaningfulness, and its linguistic structure permits software engineers to communicate ideas in less lines of code than may be conceivable in dialects like C++ or Java.

Python's key features include:

Readability: Python code is intended all things considered and decipherable, making it a magnificent language for novices and experienced engineers the same.

Extensibility: Python can be effectively reached out by incorporating with different dialects like C and C++, permitting designers to streamline basic areas of code.

Why learn Python?

Simple to Learn: Python's syntax is simple and similar to that of English, making it simple for beginners to understand programming concepts.

Flexible Applications: Python is utilized in different spaces, from web improvement (Django, Carafe) to information science (NumPy, Pandas) and man-made reasoning (TensorFlow, PyTorch).

Local area and Assets: Python has a huge and dynamic local area. There are plentiful assets, instructional exercises, and documentation accessible, making it more straightforward to learn and tackle issues.

Vocation Valuable open doors: In the job market, Python is highly sought after. Many organizations use Python for their tasks, and capability in Python can open up an extensive variety of profession valuable open doors.

Intelligibility and Viability: Python code is not difficult to peruse and keep up with, which is critical for cooperative ventures and long haul programming advancement.

Interdisciplinary Use: Python is generally utilized in logical examination, permitting researchers and scientists to zero in on tackling issues as opposed to managing complex programming language structure.

Part 2: Setting Up Your Current circumstance

2.1 Introducing Python

Before we start coding, how about we get Python introduced on your PC. You will follow the installation instructions in this chapter to ensure that you have everything you need to begin writing and running Python code.

2.2 Picking a Code Manager

A code manager is where you'll compose your Python programs. This part will acquaint you with various code editors and assist you with picking one that suits your inclinations. We'll cover well known editors like Inactive, Visual Studio Code, and Thonny.

: Greetings, World!

3.1 Composing Your Most memorable Python Program

Now is the ideal time to jump into your most memorable Python program! We will walk you through the process of writing a straightforward "Hello, World!" in this section. program. You'll gain proficiency with the fundamental design of a Python content and how to run it.

3.2 Grasping Print Explanations

The print explanation is your device for showing data in Python. We'll investigate how to utilize print to yield text and factors, and we'll examine organizing choices to make your result more discernible.

Part 2: Essential Ideas

Section 4: Factors and Information Types

4.1 Proclaiming Factors

Factors store data in your projects. This part will show you how to proclaim factors and pick fitting names for them.

4.2

Investigate the various information types in Python, like numbers for numerical activities, strings for text, and booleans for valid/misleading qualities.

Section 5: Client Information and Result

5.1 Taking Contribution from the Client

Figure out how to communicate with your projects by taking contribution from the client. We'll cover the info() capability and use it to make dynamic projects.

5.2 Organizing Result

Make your program's result more easy to use by designing text and numbers. This part will acquaint you with string designing procedures.

Section 6: Restrictive Explanations

6.1 If Explanations

Restrictive explanations assist your program with simply deciding. The if statement and how it regulates the flow of your code will be discussed in this chapter.

6.2 Else and Elif Explanations

Develop restrictive proclamations by consolidating else and elif (else-if) articulations. This permits your program to think about numerous circumstances.

Part 2: Fundamentals Chapter 7: Prologue to Circles

7.1 Involving For Circles

Present the idea of circles, zeroing in on the for circle. Figure out how to rehash a block of code a particular number of times, making your projects more proficient.

7.2 Utilizing While Circles

Investigate the while circle, an elective method for rehashing code in light of a condition. Comprehend how to make circles that run up to a specific condition is valid.

7.3 Circle Control Proclamations

Find exceptional articulations like break and proceed with that permit you to control the progression of your circles. Figure out how to leave a circle rashly or skirt specific emphasess.

Section 8: Records and Clusters

8.1 Making and Controlling Records

Present records, a strong method for putting away assortments of things. Figure out how to make, change, and access components in a rundown.

8.2 Repeating Through Records

Investigate various ways of circling through records. Learn how to use for loops to carry out actions on each item in a list.

Part 3: Capabilities and Modularization

Section 9: Prologue to Capabilities

9.1 Characterizing Capabilities

Comprehend the idea of capabilities and how they assist you with figuring out down your code into reasonable pieces. Master the art of defining your own functions.

9.2 Calling Capabilities

Investigate how to call (use) capabilities in your code. Comprehend the significance of reusable code and how works add to it.

9.3 Boundaries and Bring Articulations back

Plunge further into capabilities by figuring out how to pass data to them utilizing boundaries. Learn about the function's use of return statements.

Section 10: Scope and Worldwide Factors

10.1 Grasping Variable Degree

Dig into the possibility of variable degree and how it influences where factors can be gotten to in your code.

10.2 Worldwide versus Neighborhood Factors

Separate among worldwide and neighborhood factors. Realize when to utilize each and the effect they have on your program.

4.1 Proclaiming Factors

Grasping Factors: Learn about variables and their significance in programming.

Variable Naming Standards: Investigate the principles and best practices for naming factors.

Variable Task: Comprehend how to relegate values to factors.

Refreshing Factors: Find how to refresh the upsides of factors in your program.

Working with Strings: Know what common string operations and data are all about.

Boolean Information Type: Present the idea of boolean information types and how they are utilized for consistent activities.

5th Chapter: Client Info and Result

5.1 Taking Contribution from the Client

Utilizing the information() Capability: Figure out how to utilize the info() capability to get client input.

Switching Contribution over completely to Numbers: Handle client info and convert it into numeric information types for estimations.

5.2 Organizing Result

Print Organizing: Investigate various ways of arranging yield utilizing the print() capability.

Get away from Characters: Acquaint get away from characters with design text yield.

Part 6: Contingent Proclamations

6.1 If Articulations

Prologue to Contingent Explanations: Grasp the requirement for settling on choices in a program.

if Statement syntax: Learn how to structure Python's if statements.

Single and Different Circumstances: Investigate scenarios with one and more conditions.

6.2 Use of the Else and Elif

Statements with the Else Statements: For alternative actions, introduce the else statement.

Elif Explanations for Various Circumstances: Comprehend the elif proclamation for dealing with different circumstances in an organized way.

Part 3: Circles and Emphasis

7. 7.1 An Overview of Loops What Are Loops?

In programming, circles are structures that permit you to rehash a bunch of directions on numerous occasions. They come in handy when you want to carry out a series of actions without repeatedly writing the same code.

7.2 Why Use Circles?

Circles help in making your code more effective and lucid. They are particularly helpful while managing dull errands, for example, emphasizing through a rundown of things or executing a block of code a particular number of times.

8. Utilizing for and keeping in mind that circles

8.1 The for Circle

The for circle is utilized when you know how frequently you need to rehash a block of code. It repeats over a grouping (e.g., a rundown) and executes the block of code for every thing in the succession.

python
Duplicate code

```
for thing in grouping:
    # code to be rehashed for every thing
```

8.2 The while Circle

The while circle is utilized when you need to rehash a block of code up to a specific condition is valid. It keeps emphasizing until the condition turns out to be misleading.

python
Duplicate code

```
while condition:
```

code to be rehashed the length of the condition is valid
8.3 Model: For and while loops Let's use for and while loops to create easy examples to help you understand.

```python
Duplicate code
# Model utilizing for circle
for I in range(5):
    print("Iteration", i+1)


# Model utilizing while circle
counter = 0
while counter < 5:
    print("Iteration", counter+1)
    counter += 1
```

9. Circle Control Proclamations

9.1 The break Explanation
The break explanation is utilized to rashly leave a circle. It is much of the time utilized when a specific

condition is met, and you need to quickly stop the circle.

```python
Duplicate code
for thing in grouping:
    on the off chance that condition:
        break
    # code to be rehashed for every thing
```

9.2 The proceed with Articulation

The proceed with proclamation is utilized to skirt the remainder of the code inside a circle for the ongoing emphasis and move to the following cycle.

```python
Duplicate code
for thing in grouping:
    on the off chance that condition:
        proceed
```

    # code to be rehashed for every thing

10. Records and Exhibits

10.1 Making and Controlling Records

Records are a flexible information type in Python that can hold an arranged assortment of things. You can make, adjust, and perform different procedure on records.

python
Duplicate code

```python
my_list = [1, 2, 3, 4, 5]
my_list.append(6) # Add a thing to the furthest limit of the rundown
my_list.remove(3) # Eliminate a particular thing from the rundown
```

10.2 Repeating Through Records

Utilizing circles to repeat through records permits you to perform activities on every thing in the rundown.

```python
Duplicate code
for thing in my_list:
    print(item)
```

- Grasping capability boundaries
- Passing different boundaries
- Default boundary values

10.3 Calling Capabilities with Contentions

- Giving contentions during capability calls
- Positional and catchphrase contentions

11. Boundaries and Bring Proclamations back

11.1 Utilizing Boundaries

- How boundaries make capabilities adaptable
- Models with various boundary types

11.2 Bring Proclamations back

- What is a bring proclamation back?

- Returning qualities from a capability
- Numerous bring values back

12. Scope and Worldwide Factors

12.1 Figuring out Factor Degree
- What is variable extension?
- Neighborhood scope versus worldwide extension

12.2 Neighborhood Factors
- Factors characterized inside a capability
- Restricted degree and lifetime

12.3 Worldwide Factors
- Factors characterized external capabilities
- Getting to worldwide factors inside capabilities
- The worldwide catchphrase

12.4 Keeping away from Variable Naming Contentions

- Best practices for variable naming to stay away from clashes

- Techniques for overseeing extension really

13. Practice and Activities

13.1 Involved Activities

- Composing basic capabilities with boundaries

- Examining degree in various situations

13.2 Code Audit and Conversation

- Surveying test code with capabilities

- Examining various ways to deal with critical thinking

14. Certifiable Models

14.1 Applying Capabilities to Take care of Issues

- Involving capabilities for normal assignments
- Genuine instances of measured code

15. High level Points (Discretionary)

15.1 Lambda Capabilities
- Prologue to unknown capabilities
- Where and how to utilize lambda capabilities

15.2 Recursion
- Grasping recursive capabilities
- Recursive versus iterative methodologies

Part 5: Prologue to Articles
11. Prologue to Items and Classes
11.1 What are Items?
- Grasping the idea of items in programming
- Certifiable similarities to make sense of articles

11.2 Why Use Classes?
- The job of classes in arranging code
- Epitome and information deliberation

11.3 Making Your Top of the line
- Sentence structure for characterizing a class
- The __init__ strategy and occasion factors

12. Fundamental Knowledge of Objects

12.1 Attributes and Methods: Defining an object's attributes (properties) and its methods (functions) within a class 12.2 Instantiating Objects: Creating instances of a class and initializing object attributes Making Classes and Articles

13.1 Structure a Basic Class

- Bit by bit manual for making a fundamental class
- Adding properties and strategies to the class

13.2 Working with Numerous Items
- Making numerous occurrences of a class
- Cooperating with various items

14. Understanding Inheritance and Polymorphism 14.1 The concept of

inheritance in object-oriented programming—parent and child classes 14.2 Creating a subclass—Inheriting attributes and methods from a parent class 14.3 Overriding Methods—Modifying methods in a subclass—Customizing behavior in child classes 14.4 Polymorphism—The concept of polymorphism in OOP—Using polymorphism to write code that is flexible and reusable

15. High level Legacy Ideas

15.1 Various Legacy

- Taking care of circumstances with various parent classes
- Possible difficulties and best practices

15.2 Theoretical Classes

- Prologue to extract classes
- Characterizing theoretical strategies and their executions

Note:

This part ought to give a strong groundwork in object-situated programming (OOP) for youngsters, underscoring active models and straightforward tasks to support the ideas. Consider integrating intuitive activities and coding difficulties to make the opportunity for growth drawing in and fun.

Part 6: Straightforward Activities
Building a Straightforward Game

13.1 Presentation

Brief outline of game advancement ideas.

Significance of circles and conditionals in game rationale.

13.2 Preparing the Game Select a straightforward game concept, such as guessing or rock-paper-scissors.

Making the essential construction of the game.

13.3 Client Information and Game Rationale

Catching client input for interactivity.

Executing game rationale utilizing if articulations and circles.

Giving criticism to the client in view of their feedback.

13.4 Iterative Turn of events

Empowering iterative improvement for upgrades and new highlights.

Adding intricacy to the game as the youngster becomes agreeable.

13.5 Model: Surmise the Number

Bit by bit manual for building a "Surmise the Number" game.

Clarification of the code and how it functions.

Understanding the necessity of calculators in programming is covered in

14.1 Introduction.

Prologue to math tasks.

14.2 Configuring the Calculator

Defines the calculator program's fundamental structure.

deciding which arithmetic operations (addition, subtraction, multiplication, and division) to include.

14.3 Capabilities for Number juggling Tasks

Making separate capabilities for every number juggling activity.

Empowering modularization for better code association.

14.4 User Input for Calculations
Recording user input for the desired operation and the numbers.
Using input approval to guarantee right info.

14.5 Performing Estimations
Utilizing capabilities to perform estimations in light of client input.
Showing the outcome to the client.

14.6 Model: Straightforward Number cruncher
Walkthrough of building an essential number cruncher.
Clarification of the code and how each capability adds to the number cruncher's usefulness.

Section 6 Rundown
Support of key ideas: circles, conditionals, client information, and capabilities.

Accentuation on imagination and trial and error in game turn of events and mini-computer plan.

Basic guides to feature Pygame's abilities

18.2 Introducing and Getting everything rolling with Pygame

Introducing Pygame utilizing pip

Setting up a Pygame window and drawing fundamental components

18.3 Structure a Basic Game with Pygame

Making a fundamental game utilizing Pygame

Understanding occasion dealing with and game circles.

Part 8: Challenges and Final Projects

Chapter 17: Making Your Own Task

17.1 Picking a Task Thought

Conceptualizing project thoughts
Lining up with interests
Straightforward versus Complex undertakings

17.2 Preparation and Execution

Making a task frame
Separating errands
Setting achievements

17.3 Setting Up Your Task

Making project organizers
Rendition control essentials (for further developed clients)
Setting up your advancement climate

17.4 Coding Rules

Taking care of various tasks

18.5 Test 4: Drawing Shapes with Turtle

Executing mathematical shapes utilizing the Turtle illustrations library

Fundamental liveliness with shapes

18.6 Test 5: Intelligent Narrating

Building a straightforward intelligent story with client decisions

Utilizing contingent proclamations and circles

18.7 Test 6: Making a Plan for the day

Fostering an essential plan for the day application

Working with records and client input

Part 19: Solutions and Explanations

19.1 Understanding Solutions Overview of the Solutions Importance of Understanding Solutions 19.2 Step-by-Step Explanations In-Depth Walkthroughs of the Solutions Highlighting Key Concepts and Techniques 19.3 Optimizing Your Code Discussing Ways to Improve and Optimize Solutions Encouraging Creative Problem-Solving

Happy coding